Alligators

Victoria Blakemore

© 2017 Victoria Blakemore

All rights reserved. This book or parts thereof may not be reproduced in any form, stored in any retrieval system, or transmitted in any form by any means—electronic, mechanical, photocopy, recording, or otherwise—without prior written permission of the publisher, except as provided by United States of America copyright law. For permission requests, write to the publisher, at "Attention: Permissions Coordinator," at the address below.

vblakemore.author@gmail.com

Copyright info/picture credits

Cover, skeeze/Pixabay; Page 3, vallain/Pixabay; Page 5, paulbr75/Pixabay; Page 7, nheimstra/Pixabay; Page 9, skeeze/Pixabay; Pages 10-11, emisoo/Pixabay; Page 13, ReganE/Pixabay; Page 15, A-W-A-B/Pixabay; Page 17, Thephoenix2020/Pixabay; Page 19, skeeze/Pixabay; Page 21, skeeze/Pixabay; Page 23; FF16/Pixabay; Page 25, 12019/Pixabay; Page 27, vallain/Pixabay; Page 29, skeeze/Pixabay; Page 31, flavio10rs/Pixabay; Page 33, skeeze/Pixabay

Table of Contents

What are Alligators?	2
Size	4
Physical Characteristics	6
Habitat	8
Range	10
Diet	12
Communication	16
Movement	18
Alligator Eggs	20
Alligator Life	22
Population	24
Feeding Alligators	26
Alligators in Danger	28
Helping Alligators	30
Glossary	34

What Are Alligators?

Alligators are large reptiles. They are known for their long, armored bodies.

There are two kinds of alligators: the American alligator and the Chinese alligator. They differ in size and where they live.

The word alligator comes from the Spanish word "el lagarto," which means lizard.

Size

American alligators are the largest of the two kinds of alligators. They can grow to be about fifteen feet long and weigh over 500 pounds.

Chinese alligators are much smaller. They grow to about five feet long and weigh up to eighty pounds.

Male alligators are usually larger than female alligators.

Physical Characteristics

Alligators have a long, armored body. It is covered with bony plates called **scutes**. They are very hard and protect alligators **organs.**

Their eyes are on top of their head. They can see above the water while their body is underwater.

Their **snout** has nostrils that point up. This lets them breathe while the rest of their body is underwater.

Habitat

Alligators live in freshwater habitats. They are often found in places like lakes, swamps, ponds, marshes, and rivers.

In some places, alligators also live in **brackish** water. This is where the water is a mix of freshwater and salt water.

Range

The American alligator is found in the United States. It is seen in states like Florida and Louisiana.

Chinese alligators are only found in a small area of China. They live in the Yangtze river.

Diet

Alligators are **carnivores**.

They eat only meat.

Their diet is usually made up of birds, turtles, fish, and mammals. However, they will eat anything they can catch.

Alligators have a special **membrane** that covers their eyes when they go underwater. This protects their eyes underwater.

Alligators stay hidden in the water close to shore, then come out of the water quickly to grab prey that is near the water.

They use their strong jaws and sharp teeth to catch and eat their prey. When a tooth wears down, a new tooth will grow in to replace it.

The color of their skin helps alligators to hide from prey in the water.

Communication

Alligators use sound and movement to communicate with each other.

Alligators may charge at each other if they are angry. They may also blow bubbles or make noises under the water to communicate.

Alligators make loud bellowing sounds. Their bellows can be heard from far away. They are thought to be a way for alligators to claim their **territory**.

Movement

Alligators have a very strong tail that helps them to be very fast swimmers. Their **webbed** feet also help them to swim and wade in muddy water.

Although they are fastest in the water, alligators can run quickly for short distances.

Smaller alligators can run up to twenty-five miles per hour. Larger alligators are usually much slower.

Alligator Eggs

Alligators usually have a **clutch** of between twenty and fifty eggs.

Female alligators make a nest of grass, sticks, leaves, and mud close to the water before laying their eggs. The eggs will hatch after about two months.

The babies stay with their mother for up to two years. She protects them from predators such as bobcats, raccoons, birds, and other alligators.

Alligator Life

Large alligators are often solitary and live on their own. Smaller alligators may live together in large groups.

When the weather gets very hot or cold, alligators may dig a den. They dig it into wet mud. They don't **hibernate**, but they rest in their den.

Alligators are **cold-blooded**. They need to stay warm. They do this by laying out in the sunlight.

Population

Although the American alligator is not **endangered**, there are some areas where their population is **declining**.

The Chinese alligator is **critically endangered**. There are very few left in the wild. There are believed to be less than 150 left.

In the wild, alligators often live between 35 and 50 years. They may live even longer in **captivity**.

Feeding Alligators

Some people like to feed alligators. This is very dangerous for people and alligators.

If alligators are fed by people, they may start to think of people when they think of food. They may become more **aggressive** when they are near people.

ALLIGATORS
MAY LIVE HERE

BE GATOR SAFE:
Do Not Approach, Feed or Harass Alligators

<u>Warning</u>: It is UNLAWFUL to feed alligators!

Feeding, harassing, or the unlawful killing or taking of alligators can result in substantial fines and/or jail time.

A fed alligator loses its natural fear of humans. This can pose a danger to the public, and ultimately results in the alligator's death.

REMEMBER
A FED GATOR IS A DEAD GATOR!

Report violations to:
SC Department of Natural Resources
24 hours a day at 1-800-922-5431
www.dnr.sc.gov

DNR

Alligators in Danger

Alligators are facing several big threats. The main threat is that their habitats are being destroyed.

In some places, alligators are hunted for their skin and their meat. When too many are hunted, populations could be in trouble.

Alligators that come into areas too close to people may be in danger.

Helping Alligators

American alligators were once **endangered**. They were hunted for their meat and skin. Now there are laws that protect them from hunting.

There are also areas like the Everglades National park that are protected habitats for animals like alligators.

Chinese alligators are still in trouble. Groups like the Wildlife Conservation Society of China are trying to help them.

They are raising alligators in **captivity**. They teach the alligators how to survive in the wild so they can be released. They want to prevent them from becoming **extinct**.

Glossary

Aggressive: mean, unfriendly, ready to fight

Brackish: water that is a mix of salt water and fresh water

Captivity: animals that are kept by humans, not in the wild

Carnivore: an animal that eats only meat

Clutch: eggs laid at the same time

Cold-Blooded: an animal whose temperature changes with the air temperature

Critically Endangered: nearly extinct

Declining: getting smaller

Endangered: at risk of becoming extinct

Extinct: when there are no more of an animal left in the wild

Hibernate: when an animal sleeps through the winter

Membrane: a thin layer of tissue

Organs: parts of the body that have a special job, such as the heart or lungs

Scutes: hard, bony plates in an alligator's skin

Snout: the front part of an animals head that sticks out, includes the nose, mouth, and jaw

Territory: an area of land that an animal clams as its own

Webbed: joined by a web

About the Author

Victoria Blakemore is a first grade teacher in Southwest Florida with a passion for reading.

You can visit her at

www.elementaryexplorers.com

Also in This Series